D0195886

Never Stop Shutting Up

A Book of Advice and Other Things

You Didn't Ask For

Mike Falzone

NEVER STOP SHUTTING UP. Copyright © 2012 Mike Falzone.

All rights reserved.

ISBN 978-1-105-75706-8

CONTENTS

Never Stop Shutting Up

A Book of Advice and Other Things

You Didn't Ask For

Mike Falzone

Forward by Craig D'Andrea

     Meeting Mike Falzone was just like watching the first twenty minutes of Freddy Got Fingered. It was plain fucking awful. The main difference is that Freddy also got funny. I hate Mike Falzone.

How To Get Dumped

It's really fuckin' easy to get broken up with. Trust me, I've done it a bunch. There are tons of reasons you may be getting broken up with (even as we speak). Whether or not you know it you may be a liar, a cheater, a manipulator, a bitch, an asshole, or simply not *the one*. Sometimes your actions get you dumped. You may say something stupid, you may commit some sort of adulterous act, you may adopt a baby without telling the person you are with. Whatever the case may be, you've been broken up with, and you are starting a new life (for the time being), alone.

Let's say that you don't see this break-up coming. How do you deal with the instant change of pace? The sleepless nights? The uncontrollable subconscious thoughts? Maybe you have to see this person again soon in school or at work. What do you do? You follow these vaguely helpful steps to coping with your brand new heartbreak and you get ready to love your life again. Because just like your late relationship, your unhappiness will end.

Step One

Calmly voice your disappointment with the untimely ending of your relationship. Don't yell. Don't get upset. Don't swear. Simply say something like, "I wish this could have worked out some other way," or "I'm sad to see this end and I wish you the best." This lets the person know that you are recognizing and attempting to understand their choice to end the relationship. Very mature of you, if I do say so myself.

Step Two

Do NOT date or hook up with someone in a childish attempt to get back at the person who just broke up with you. This is a classic/desperate/transparent move and you're not fooling anyone. Your life is not about making people jealous. Plus, you run the risk of hurting more people in the process. And why? Because you feel sad? Don't bring other people into your world of shit.

Step Three

The best thing you can do is start having a much fun as humanly possible. This DOES NOT mean going out and getting fucked up. I repeat, do NOT get fucked up. Drunken nights end in drunken fights. Drinking begets drunk texts and phone calls which never end the way you think they will. Look at that. Me giving you the benefit of the doubt by implying that you have thought out the end game to your drunken communication. You haven't. It's not going to end well. You've just been dumped, and depending on how upset you are, you probably have nothing but bad ideas. You're gonna have to trust me for a minute. I'm trying to help you.

Go out and have an amazing experience with yourself. Go skydiving (with a parachute... wiseass) for charity. Do something productive, something that may help someone else. Do something selfless and let the person who just broke your heart find out about it. (Yeah, it's passive aggressive. Would you rather be sad and locked away in your room for a month? Or passive aggressive with a sense of accomplishment? It's the lesser of two evils.) Not because you told them, or had someone else tell them, but because it was truly great and a positive step for you as a human being.

Step Four

Spend a day or two upset. You deserve it. You are allowed to be sad, but for a limited time only. Don't try to get him or her back, because what you are really doing is attacking yourself. Least attractive quality a love interest could have: Not wanting you back.

In breaking your heart, this person just freed you up to meet the love of your life.

5 Best Places to Score a Free Tee Shirt

1. College

2. Any event that ends in "A-Thon"

3. Bars with trivia nights

4. Minor League hockey games

5. Any business with a radio station van parked outside

How To Fuck With a Bully's Head

Bullying is very easy to understand. The difference between being a bully and getting bullied is a race to see who recognizes whose insecurity first. However, understanding what drives a bully doesn't make it suck any less– it hurts to be made fun of. Depending on which stage of development you're in, it can even scar you for life. Being bullied makes you feel alone (even if you are with a group of people; you are still being singled out, you're being hurt, you're alone), and no one likes to be alone. As human beings, we are the most vulnerable when we're alone. Naked and without shelter, we encounter hurtful words and sometimes physical pain on our way to being comfortable with who we are.

I was made fun of on and off throughout my childhood. I was pretty cool up through fourth grade. I got a free pass on being an idiot by being funny. By the time fifth and sixth grade rolled around I had become "chubby" and took on all of the jibber jabber that goes along with that. Then for whatever reason, I was fucking awesome in seventh and eight grade. I was going to parties, kissing girls, and going out with the girl with the biggest boobs in middle school (until she cheated on me with this kid Adam. I haven't truly forgiven either of them.)

High school was a little different. I gained and lost weight bi-weekly. I was fat, then I wasn't, then I was and so it went until graduation. I had man-boobs, still kinda do, which was always something to poke fun off. I was the typical guy that every girl was friends with, but no one wanted to date. I played music and made my own CDs but was called names by most of the people who caught wind of my entrepreneurial endeavors. I was the kid who made all of the sports teams, but rarely made it into any of the actual games. By doing so, I earned the name Struggles Falzone, a name that has followed to this day in some circles. Long story short, I was bursting with insecurity and there were plenty of people who had no problem pointing all of them out.

Over time I learned to appreciate how awesome I was. That sentence is SO much easier to type than it was/is to live. When the people you *think* you should be respecting are making fun of you, you start to wonder what is wrong with you. Truth is, there is nothing wrong with you. You are simply different enough to be pointed out and thus... bullied.

If you get fed up enough you are going to do one of two things: give up, or stand up for yourself. Sadly, way too many people give up.

As I see it, there are three main ways to fuck with a bully's head. You can fight them, you can develop your own form of peaceful resistance, or you can strike back (verbally) in a hurtful way and never look back. Each way comes with its limitations– there is no foolproof way to get through being bullied unscathed. Think of it like this: if you put your hands up to block a punch, it's still going to hurt, but if you're lucky, it may hurt less than getting hit.

Let's be blunt. You *could* fight your bully. You could clench your fists and gather up all of the adolescent rage in your quivering little body and you can just keep punching until the hurt goes away. In *theory*, you can. In reality, whether you win or lose, the hurt won't go away. In reality, you'll get punched in the fucking face and that sucks. Being bullied hurts enough, and if you aren't already getting hit, you don't need to add that to your emotional pain.

Fights don't have the glamorous schmaltz they do in the movies or did in the 20's. You can't just gather the school around the playground, strike a furious, *David versus Goliath*-type blow and have that be that. Today retaliation is king and fights are never really just between two people... and they're also never really over for that matter. Fighting is out of the question unless someone is physically attacking you. Then rules become feckless.

Peaceful resistance is always the method of choice for the noble, and if you are lucky enough to be raised as a good person, this is the method for you. In my mind, some of the strongest images ever captured have been those of peaceful resistance over the course of history. Sitting quietly and seemingly unaffected by the turmoil around you is an amazing feat that is both beautiful and empowering. That being said, it's also one of the hardest things in the world to pull off.

As with anything else I've ever tried to do, I can't help but slip a little bit of *smart-ass* into the equation. Should you find yourself testing the peaceful resistance method, try to do it with a smile. Smiles tend to fuck with people's heads. You always want to know what the smiling kid is thinking about. What makes you happier than me, *smiling kid?* Why should you be happy? I'm making fun of you, what's your problem? You're so weird! Seriously stop, you're freaking me out!

Mission accomplished.

My grandfather's name was Efstratious Chocas. Did you ever hear a Greek-er name than Efstratious Chocas? It's almost sounds like a Greco magic spell when you say it slowly. When we were out in public, people used to come up to my grandfather and congratulate him for creating math. That's how Greek he was. He had this move he loved to do when we were driving. Whenever someone would beep at him or flip him off, he would just smile and wave. One day I asked him why he would do such a thing. Why not get mad? Why not step on the gas, follow them to their house, and beat them with one of the many golf clubs you have in your trunk?

"If you wave and smile, they think you're senile," Grandpa said.

He was a better man than I could ever be.

That leaves us with the way I chose to handle my problems in high school: words. When I decided to stand up for myself, I discovered that I had a way with words. Cynical, sarcastic, and sometimes disgusting words. I was sick of getting picked on and lied to.

What's a boy to do? Well, first you find out what makes the other person really, *really* sad. You call them out and you don't look back. I was never strong enough to fight and I was never docile enough to let it roll off my back. I had to do something. I would do research on the people who hurt me. I would find out which of them had stuffed bras, alcoholic parents, pregnancy scares, weird scars, clubbed feet, webbed toes, and anything else I could conjure up. The gloves were off– these people had hurt me so I was going to show them exactly how that felt. I lashed out quickly (comic timing is really important) and effectively. Sometimes I got hit, sometimes I got sent to the office, sometimes my parents would hear me say disgusting things and I would feel ashamed, but after a certain point I couldn't help but stick up for myself.

Things have come full circle for me, personally. I am finally man enough to let things go, instantly. Words don't bother me like they used to and I'm not filled with the same hostility that I once was. People say things, I hear them (or read them), and then they are gone. That didn't come over night. Sometimes you have to deal with things in dumb ways in order to recognize the smartest course of action.

Time will go by and you'll realize that you are too awesome to let small things bother you. This is going to sound a bit glib but the truth of the matter is, all of us are alone... and that's not necessarily a bad thing. You were given a life by your parents, and (whether they are around or not) it's up to you, by yourself, to go forth and make the best of it. Make other people smile by making yourself happy and you'll do all right.

Bullying does a lot of different things: it sucks, it hurts, but it also ends. But it doesn't end because a bully says it does. It ends because you say it does. Bullying is nothing but insecure people recognizing their own lack of self-confidence in you. No one's insecurities are ever going to just disappear, but there are ways to guard it.

Some people choose to guard their insecurity with sarcasm, muscles, or eye makeup. But the strongest possible defense is self-confidence: the knowledge that you are your own unique self, and the pride you have in that fact. Confidence doesn't come overnight. It's not something you can wish for before you go to bed and take to school the next day. Confidence comes through getting hurt and rejected enough to understand how amazing you are.

You're awesome. I promise.

How to Get Kicked Out of a Band: Part One: NYC

For a few years I was lucky enough to be in a band with two of my best friends. The lineup would change from time to time, players would come and go, but the three of us would make music for the better part of four years. Jim played drums, James played bass and sang harmonies, and I played guitar and sang lead. This band, like many others, started in an assortment of basements. We would write music, practice, and play live without much direction. I won't to get into the history of the band, our day-to-day interaction with each other, our ups and down, etc. That's not what this book is about. This book is focused on funny things that take up a page or two at a time.

Some advice, from me to you: Should you find yourself in a band with two of your best friends... break up. We had some amazing times together. We were able to travel together, open up for nationally touring acts, record an album, and act ridiculous in public time and time again. I wouldn't trade those times for anything in the world. But that being said, I truly believe that the only reason we are still close friends is because we stopped playing music with each other. When we weren't laughing until we were unable to speak, we were despising each other so deeply that you could taste the hatred in the back of the throat.

The band's "trying times" came as a direct result of spinning our wheels professionally. We would bust our asses and empty our wallets in the studio to make a record we wrote in a basement to play for empty rooms. This is a common problem with bands in general. Once you have an audience you can play anywhere and do anything. We thought that all we had to do was play live... constantly. People would hear how *amazing* we were and just keep showing up. They would have no choice. Every weekend. For four years. Right?

We somehow landed an unofficial residency at this place called Uncle Mike's in Tribeca. In our minds, if we were playing in New York City consistently, we were doing something right. The weird thing about being from Connecticut is that if you tell people you have a band, the first question you get back is "DO YOU PLAY IN THE CITY?!" I guess this residency was just our excuse to say yes.

Uncle Mike's is a typical NYC dive bar. It smelled like they never washed the floor or cleaned the bathrooms. I read an article once about them having rats, but the rodents seemed to fit in with the regulars so I don't think anyone really minded.

One of the things that made Uncle Mike's unique was the fact that it is right next to a strip club. On their nights off from the club, the dancers would tend bar at Uncle Mike's. They would always be dressed in some stereotypical, sexy Halloween costume. In the course of a year I saw a lot of sexy kittens, slutty nurses, and countless Wonder Women tend bar.

We started playing there in October so we thought it was seasonal, but it wasn't. It was the dress code.

Appearances aside, the manager loved us, the bartenders were always uber-nice, and the promoters welcomed us with open arms, no matter how far under the twenty-five person minimum draw we were. Whether we liked it or not, Uncle Mike's was our second home.

Promoters had a nasty habit of cramming as many bands as possible into any given night at the bar, yet it was commonplace to not see the soft glow of the stage lights until 1am. No matter what time our set was we would religiously arrive around 9pm. I take full responsibility for the obnoxiousness and the animosity this caused. It was my understanding that if we were not on time, we would be seen as unprofessional.

Unbeknownst to me, no one ever gave a fuck about when we showed up. Lesson learned. We'd show up, load in, get drunk, wait for the hangover to set in, and then play. We were always there THAT long.

This particular night was no different. There were a ton of other bands on the bill and we were slated to go on last. The three of us got to the bar early, ordered our usual (three shots of your worst tequila... heated up) and waited to play. Shitty band after shitty band played way over their allotted time as about twenty of our friends trickled in (a fine turnout indeed).

The bar was unusually packed that night. There was rarely a good crowd at Uncle Mike's, and we figured something was wrong. As the night went on we came to learn that a high school band would be performing right before us. This was one of their first shows, which explained the turnout. People have this habit of supporting the shit out of their friends when their band is new and shiny.

The high schoolers took the stage at midnight, roughly an hour after their scheduled set time. By this point, our audience grew restless and was looking for any excuse to leave. The high schoolers started to play some crudely written songs with instruments and chords which they had probably acquired less than a month prior. Thus, a great excuse to leave. Two by two, our friends started to depart. I both sympathized with them and loathed them for having a way out, as I stood there seething with my two band mates. We were sick of this happening week after week.

I remember one particularly touching moment where James' aunt (age fifty-something), who had stayed out WAY past her bedtime, turned to James and said, "I... I just have to go sweetie." Right then the three of us made a pact to get drunk (again) and play louder then we ever had before out of spite. There was but one problem: The high schoolers were still very much on stage. Now running long by more than fifteen minutes.

As we became delirious with fatigue and hatred, we began to deal with our delirium in our own individual ways. Jim, having been sick and awake since 6am for work, started drinking half-finished beers lying on and around the bar. I remember saying, "Dude you're gonna get sick, that's gross." To which he replied, "I'm already sick. I'm not going to get *more* sick!"

"Fair point," I said, and left him alone to finish. We were, after all, on our second round of being drunk. Who was I to tell anyone how to live his life at this point?

James was standing in the middle of the disparagingly upbeat crowd. His eyes were glazed over, he was audibly gritting his teeth, and teetering at the edge of what it was to act civilized in public. He seemed to be waiting for a trigger to send him over the edge, and he got it. Upon ending yet another drab musical selection, the band uttered the words that would send James spiraling toward temporary insanity.

"Ok, we got two more songs for ya!" the prepubescent teenager squealed with an innocence that seemed to tell the world: *I have no idea what stage etiquette is.*

Unable to control himself, James cupped his hand around him mouth and yelled, "IF YOU PLAY TWO MORE SONGS, I WILL FUCKING KILL YOU."

Things became significantly more interesting at that moment: the place fell silent. At one moment the audience was beaming with pride from seeing their friends play in the best city in the world and the next, their attention was turned to James. They were confused. Before James could even finish the breath he had been using to berate the teenagers, he was being pursued. Uncle Mike's had an army of menacing-looking bouncers. Our personal favorite was a Hispanic gentleman on the shorter side, known specifically for wearing brass knuckles and a Bluetooth headset at all times. I watched in horror from the bar as "Bluetooth" made a beeline for my bass player. James had no idea what was coming, having had his back turned to the imminent danger that approached.

With every audience member Bluetooth shoved out of his way, he charged closer to his target. He seemed to be licking his lips with anticipation. Almost like he had been waiting for an excuse to beat the shit out of someone. Enter James. Bluetooth reached out to grab James and I turned around and ordered another shot of tequila.

In a delightful turn of events that no one could have foreseen, the bouncer was intercepted at the zero hour by the lead singer's mother. The next ten minutes were filled with this lioness tearing into James' flesh with her words.

"HOW DARE YOU THREATEN MY BOY. YOU ARE THE WORST PERSON I'VE EVER MET!" ...so on and so forth. Jim met me at the bar for a drink. We watched and waited for it to be over. What could we do? I remember James saying something to the effect of, "Welcome to New York City." Welcome indeed.

James was removed from the establishment until we took the stage. When he returned I guess I was expecting some sort of apology. I reminded him that I never had to worry about situations like this when I was a solo act. He then called me a pussy for not sticking up for our band. We are different, James and me. We loaded out and took the FDR to head home. That night, for the first time, I told him I no longer wanted to play music with him. He told me to go fuck myself and nodded off until I dropped him off at home.

He was back in the band a week later.

7 Things Six Year-Olds Usually Smell Like

1. Syrup

2. Halloween candy

3. Chewable vitamins

4. Johnson and Johnson

5. Carpet swatches

6. Car seats

7. Blocks

Firsts

If there is one thing I have learned through my many hours of talking into a camera by myself, it's that if you talk to yourself long enough, you just may accidentally *fascinate* yourself. The last time I was the victim of accidental fascination was on a recent trip to Doylestown, PA.

Doylestown is one of my favorite places of all time. The houses are rustic and close together, Mom-and-Pop shops line the streets, there are crossing guards at every corner ("Thank *goodness*," says the guy walking while looking into a camera), and though I'm sure it has, I've never once seen it rain. I have heard it rain, but I have never seen water actually fall from the sky and hit the ground in Doylestown. Not once. None of this has anything to do with the "Firsts" concept, I just wanted to bring you all there with me. For the next twenty minutes or so, I will be mentally walking though Doylestown.

I am fascinated by firsts. The first time something happens it's new and fresh and exciting and clumsy and scary and a bunch of other things all at the same time. People are obsessed with sharing stories about their first time with a new experience. Sex, school, ice cream, fights, kissing, peeing in public; all of these stories are interesting because they deal with something that was recently unknown to us. Were you scared? Nervous? I was! Let me tell you about it! Oh please do!

As I was walking through D-town to grab a cup of coffee I began to let my un-caffeinated mind drift. I remembered the first time I had a cup of coffee. I was at a family party. My cousins and I were sneaking around the house and pretending we were GI Joes (or some similar bullshit). We set little missions for ourselves, Operation: Make the Dog Slide Around the Kitchen After Spraying the Floor with Pam. Stuff like that. I remember a coffee-themed mission at one point. Being a dedicated solder, I remember sneaking into the kitchen, pouring myself a cup, spilling a little, burning myself, tasting the coffee, hating it, and watching the adults drink cup after cup without so much as a hiccup. How did they do that? That stuff was gross. Fast-forward twenty years later and I can't function as a human without a cup of coffee in the morning. Firsts.

One of my favorite things about being a comic is that there are a few different ways to make people laugh. You can either say something completely logical and identify with your audience, or you can throw all logic aside and just speak. On my little coffee jaunt through Doylestown, I did both. Here is what I came up with:

The First Baby

Whether you believe in evolution or Creation, there had to be a "first human." That human being was at one point, the "first baby." I suppose it is more logical to picture this person as the product of an evolving being, a gradual process resulting in fully the functional being we recognize today. But I choose to entertain the idea of the First Baby.

In my mind, one day there was just a human baby. Naked, hungry, crying, alone, rocking side to side in the grass, just trying to survive. What was the daily struggle like for this baby? Babies are SO easily breakable. How did it brave the elements? How did the first baby learn to live off of the land? On its daily routine of rocking side to side (unaware of the possibility and incapable of standing on its own), did it land its tiny baby mouth on some crushed berries or leaves? Was this what kept the first baby alive long enough to develop into the first toddler and so on? Did the first baby say to itself, "Hmm, I ate that berry and I didn't die today. I think I'll try the same thing tomorrow. Let's see how long we can keep this thing going. Also, I now know what a berry is and I have named it as such."

The First Rapper

I would imagine the first rappers were simply a group of people trying to rehearse for *Shakespeare in the Park* while the first garage band practiced down the street. Eventually, talent and structure was brought into the rap game.

The First Sneeze

The first person to sneeze must have been convinced their brain had exploded. Furthermore, the person next to the inaugural sneezer must have been equally scared.

"What the hell was that? Why did you yell at me really fast? Are you going to do it again? Did your nose just throw up?"

The First "Bro"

The term *bro* is now, unfortunately, a fully functioning member of the casual greeting family. I want to know about the first time the *bro* was used to address someone who wasn't related to the speaker. How confused must this person have been– perhaps he was expecting a "Hello Stephen," or "Hello old friend," but never in a million years would he have expected a "What's up bro?" from someone who was not of relation.

What about the speaker? Let's call him Thad. Why would Thad use the term "bro?" Perhaps Stephen resembled his brother. Perhaps the setting was dimly lit and it was merely a case of mistaken identity? Perhaps upon overhearing Thad's mistake, a more popular patron of the establishment took "bro" and ran with it? Who knows for sure? No one... cool story.

The First Person to Take Medicine

This thought haunted me for years. Who was the first person to try medicine? How sick do you have to be to pour some other person's educated guess down your gullet? Maybe people were forced to try medicine?

EXT. MEDIEVAL PHARMACY (BETA VERSION) – MID DAY

PHARMACIST:

Oh, we'll try the new batch out on Jacob!

ASSISTANT:

Why Jacob?

PHARMACIST:

He's incredibly sick. Close to death, he is. This could be the very thing that cures him! And *we'll* be responsible for saving this man's life!

ASSISTANT:

But what if it doesn't work?

PHARMACIST:

Then nothing will change for anyone involved. It's not like he's going to get sicker.

ASSISTANT:

Well, actually– he might.

PHARMASIST:

Oh, yeah. He might.

Poor, desperate Jacob. I just want him to be okay.

I wonder if, because of poor record keeping technology, the pharmacist completely forgot what some of his concoctions were even made of.

"YOU CAN WALK NOW? REALLY? Shit, what was in that one?"

The First Sarcasm

There are a few super-fun ways to think about this one. Being an incredibly sarcastic person myself, I have played this scenario out in my head thousands of times. There is no telling when sarcasm actually started, but it is safe to say that it had to be well after a language was established and mastered. I'd like to believe that sarcasm started with the cavemen.

FADE IN

EXT. ROCKS SURROUNDING CAMP FIRE – NIGHT

Two cavemen sit and eat a wildebeest they had hunted and
killed earlier that afternoon.

CAVEMAN ONE:

Hey, how is your wildebeest?

CAVEMAN TWO:

(Sarcastic)

Great. Yeah, it's *really* great wildebeest.

CAVEMAN ONE:

(Confused)

Oh. Great.

They eat in silence for a moment.

CAVEMAN TWO:

You know, it's not really that great... the wildebeest meat. It's actually kind of undercooked.

CAVEMAN ONE:

(Perplexed)

Oh... then why would you say it was great?

CAVEMAN TWO cocks his head to the side and thinks about his response.

CAVEMAN TWO:

I don't know. I guess I was being...

(Pauses)

...Something.

SCENE

How to Get Kicked Out of a Band: Part Two: Cape Cod

After months upon months of only minor daily conflict, we remained a band. The boys and I were spinning our wheels tirelessly every weekend in search of our childhood dreams. Travel became a top priority for us. Sure, we could get twenty people out to a show in Connecticut and New York, but could we sway our massive fan base to Massachusetts?

January is cold in the Northeast. I don't live in Canada or Antarctica so I'm being a bit of a puss-basket when I say, "I'm freezing," but nevertheless, I was. We had been invited by a local family band to play with them at a small restaurant on the Cape. "Why not make a weekend of it?" we thought, and we booked a show in Boston for the night after. I don't remember much of that day. I'm sure it was similar to any other semi-enthusiastic band trip we had ever taken. We'd meet up, the keyboard and bass player would show up an hour late, we'd leave, and drive in quiet resentment to our destination. We resented each other a lot.

Two and a half hours later we had arrived in Cape Cod. Crossing the bridge onto the cape, I had imagined the car mighty-morphing into a minivan, windows down, kids prematurely dawning swimmies, mother applying suntan lotion, dad at the reins of the family chariot, but alas... it was fucking January. The small town might as well have been settled on an iceberg floating adrift at sea or better yet, on Jupiter. There was no one to be found anywhere. I remember needing to stop for gas at some point and I thought to myself, "Welp, better start drilling!"

At one point Jim (on drums, ladies and gentlemen) needed sticks. We ran into a closing music store and ended up meeting this guy named Zee. Zee was apparently elated with the fact that an original band came to play the tundra and took a liking to Jim right away. I guess Zee, a heavyset, bearded, biker-looking rock god, was somewhat of a local celebrity and played drums with several acts of note. I can't remember a single one. He sold Jim two overpriced sets of sticks, made Jim watch him play drums for twenty minutes, then showed us a small venue he helped run across the street. The place held about one hundred and fifty people or so, sort of a dive, but not really. They had a really nice speaker system and *thousands* of dollars-worth of LED lighting that would seem out of place just about anywhere. We would have loved to play that place, but no, we were at the frozen crab shack down the street.

We were greeted by the evening with a cold slap in the teeth. As we pulled into the venue-slash-restaurant street parking, we were greeted the by local family band. There were two sisters (I think), a father and son (I think), and one super-nice guy I had gone to college with, who had invited us to come up and play in the first place. We exchanged small talk for a bit, asked each other about our corresponding trips, sorted out the financial situation for the evening, and began to unload. This is important: I do not remember exactly how much money we were promised. I don't think it was an exact amount, I think it was a percentage of what the bar made, which was to be split between both bands.

The family band set up their stuff first, being the headlining act and all, and we set our stuff up in front of them. It was tight and uncomfortable and everything we were used to.

For whatever reason, James (bass) went through this phase where he would just spit, constantly. Inside, outside, public bathrooms, on stage, it didn't matter where we were. The kid was like a fucking cartoon camel. I never understood it. I would scold him like an old-school teacher and it would only prompt him to spit more out of spite. Fucking saliva fountain he was. I remember him spitting on the "stage," or more accurately, the designated area in which we were to stand. I scolded him in close proximity to the microphone, which drew only negative attention to the situation. No way to spin this one. One of the members of the invited out of town band was spitting all over the floor of your restaurant...sorry.

We played a jazzy version of our set for the people who were still shucking their out-of-season seafood delights, then turned up the volume and played the exact same songs again as they were written. That was one of our favorite pastimes, though volume was a consistent argument factor within the band. The family band played to what appeared to be members of the extended family, and boy could that family drink. The bartenders were busy all night, people were up and dancing, and everything seemed to be going as planned.

The family band finished their set and was met with thunderous applause from the twenty-five members of the extended family that made up the audience. We started to load up our gear and as we did, the restaurant started to clean up and close out.

Outside, we stared, mesmerized by the clouds of smoke our breath made against the dead night air, thinking how much more packed this show would have been if it had been warmer. We were completely packed up and ready to settle up with the family band. Through the window I saw a few members of the family band surrounding the bartenders who were dividing up cash. Being the bandleader, I figured I should be a part of this. I tried to enter the bar, but the door was locked. Interesting.

I knocked, no answer. I knocked louder. A half-annoyed female member of the family band answered the door and told me to wait with my band outside. She shut the door in my face. I turn around to face my band mates, who were safely out of earshot. All they had seen was another band dividing money with the bar, me attempting to join the party and being snubbed at the door like a guy who had come to the hottest club in town with twenty other dudes.

"What the fuck was that?!" James barked loudly across the frosty deserted island.

I mumbled something back, freezing, tired, annoyed. Much like in New York City, James saw me as the "pussy band leader."

"Are they fucking stiffing us?" James asked.

"No, everything is fine, just shut up and wait a second," I said in a reassuring tone.

"Fuck this, I'm cold, get our money so we can get the fuck out of here!"

James had this habit of being very adamant about leaving when he wanted to leave. We once played a show to no one at a college in Maine. After the show we went to a killer party, and after the party we went to this girl's dorm room. One of the girls called James "Just the bass player" (which I remind him of to this day) and took an interest in making out with me... eventually. I sat with this girl on her bed talking about nothing in particular until James busted in at 3 am screaming, "GIVE ME THE KEYS, I'M FUCKING DRIVING HOME!" We did. James would them kick and scream his way to the car and fall asleep instantly while I drove home, hence the birth of one of his many nicknames: Sweet Baby James.

Again I tried to calm James down, but I knew I wasn't going to have any luck. He frantically looked around the barren, ice-covered streets of Cape Cod. There were only four or five cars around. Ours, the family band van, a Corvette owned by the husband of one of the female singers, and a van owned by the mother of the family band.

"I'm gonna go steal that car," James said, pointing to the Corvette, which was running and unlocked to warm up a bit in the icy abyss.

"Don't... idiot," I said, knowing it was going to happen anyway.

"Yeah... That's what I'm gonna do. SWEET VETTE BRO!"

James then assured us that he wasn't going to *steal* it, but move it up the street so it appeared to be stolen. Everyone thought it would be hilarious. I even giggled for a second, remembering that our money for the evening was inside a warm building and we were not. The kid I went to college with came out to meet me in the middle of the street, handed me a fraction of what we thought we were getting that night, and walked back into the restaurant.

James has this saunter he does when he is really mad, or *really* sure of himself. He did that over to this running, unlocked Corvette. He palmed the handle and opened the door.

"STOP! THEIF!" cried the band mother, who had watched the entire thing unfold from the comfort of the family van. I'm not sure what she said after that. She ran up to James screaming bloody murder, then ran back into the van, then into the restaurant. We didn't know it then but the mother had closed her finger in the van door and was bleeding.

Imagine what must have been running through the collective mind of the family band: There is an out-of-town band waiting outside for money, they are in the process of stealing our car and now my mother is bleeding. James got out of the car and sauntered back to us as if to say, "Yup. That JUST happened." The car sat behind him, running and unlocked as if nothing had ever happened at all.

"You're an idiot and I hate you," I think I said to James while the mother went to alert the family of the grand theft auto that was happening outside. At that moment the lights in the restaurant went out and there was a constant ringing of drunk female yelling all around.

"Let's get the fuck out of here," we seemed to say in unison.

We got to our cars and took off down the street when my cell phone starting blowing up. It was the kid I had gone to college with. He was not happy. The following is a transcription from memory of how the phone conversation went:

ME: Hello?

COLLEGE GUY: YEAH FUCK YOU, HELLO! (Loud

yelling) ...STEALING MY FUCKING

BROTHER'S CAR (phone fumbling and more yelling)
KICK YOUR FUCKING ASSES (more

loud yelling followed by softer female voice yelling in
the background) YEAH... I'M TELLING 'EM NOW.
FUCK YOU ASSHOLE!

My heart sank. This poor kid invited us to play with his band at the Cape. We came up, spit all over his stage, "attempted to steal a car," then booked as their bleeding mother recounted the story to them in the freezing cold. I had to at least attempt to rectify the situation.

ME: Dude... DUDE. Turn around and meet me back at the

restaurant. I'll give you back your money.

As soon as I hung up the phone James called me a pussy. There are times in our friendship where I truly felt like James was sorry that he was associated with me in any way. Right or wrong, this was one of those times.

We turned around, I gave the family band back the pathetic bit of money they had awarded us for standing out in the cold for so long, and stood motionless and defeated on the icy sidewalk.

"FAGGOT," my college friend yelled as they sped away.

I got in the car, looked at James, and said, "I'm sick of you." We drove in silence to Boston that night, contemplating the future of the band. We got to a friend's apartment and I slept restlessly on a couch covered in white dog fur. Then next morning we woke up, had a band meeting, broke up for three hours, went to get pancakes and played our Boston show night and every weekend for two years after that.

Conversation Starters for Hipsters

I can't be sure if I've actually heard these or not. But if I close my eyes, and quietly transport myself to a dark bar in Williamsburg, it's hard *not* to hear these hipster conversation starters.

"Hey, where'd you get that vest?"

"Do you know where I can get a decent vegan burger at 3 am?"

"Tell me about your fedora-tracking smartphone app idea again."

"I heard Bud heavy was the new PBR."

"How much I enjoy a bar is directly related to the amount of exposed brick I can see."

"I heard Rheingold is making a light beer."

"You started sewing your old shirts together and selling them as table cloths on Etsy?!"

"How hard is it to do a Magic Eye with those glasses on?"

"I heard your cat has a three-syllable first name..."

"No, I don't listen to indie rock anymore... just indie."

"My new band has sort of a *Pre-Jazz* feel to it."

"Sometimes I feel like fashion is going backwards and I'm
    okay with that."

"Dude, I really like that messenger bag."

"I love my bike, but if I ever get a car it will totally be
    environmentally friendly."

"I disagree...Bon Iver's record has at least four genres on it."

"This shirt has a Capital V-neck."

"I'm just so over the way deodorant makes me feel."

"I just got a new compost bin for my kitchen counter."

15 Things You Learn In Pre-School That Will Eventually Kill You

Sharing

Sharing is all well and good when it pertains to crayons and chalk, but not so much when it comes to communicable diseases.

Following People to the Bathroom

As you grow older, you'll find that your peers enjoy a certain mount of space when it comes to matters of the bathroom. This, of course, does not include groups of girls. Girls love to follow each other to the bathroom to watch each other dispense of waste and share secrets. Keep in mind that sharing the wrong secret can get you killed; also watch out for dysentery and other diseases.

Lines

Standing in line is an easy way to organize children... or prisoners. The older you are, the less likely you should be to find yourself in a line. I am reminded of the old saying: Like a lamb to the slaughter. I'd imagine the lambs in a line. Don't line up, nothing good is going to happen.

Nap Time

Naps are the shit. Take as many naps as humanly possible. Just don't do it the same way you did in preschool, i.e. with large groups of people. Sleeping with many people at once will eventually kill you. Obvious sexually transmitted disease overtones aside, group sleeping or *slouping* is unsafe at best. Should you wake up and find yourself in a *slouping* situation, quickly identify your surroundings, (you are probably in a homeless shelter or a prison) then leave.

Getting Someone Else to Unbutton Your Pants

Buttons are super tough to a child. It's like solving a Rubik's cube every time you have to take a piss. A helping hand is needed from time to time in order to avoid accidents, but try not to ask for the same kind of assistance through your adolescent years. If you are physically capable of unbuttoning your own pants, you should keep that job to yourself. Ask the wrong person for help and they may kill you.

Trusting Creepy Adults

Unless they are working at the gift shop in Disney World, I wouldn't trust the grown man in the Mickey Mouse sweater. Chances are this guy has a van and doesn't have a band or soccer-playing offspring to justify it. You're going to get kidnapped and this guy is going to stop the progression of your life. Don't make eye contact, and keep moving. If he should address you in some way, pretend to be on your phone or in the middle of a sneeze that won't come out.

Thinking That It's Okay To Hug Dinosaurs

Most of the kids that came out of the mid to late 80's and 90's are familiar with Barney the purple dinosaur. Barney taught us that it was okay to trust, hug, learn from, and sing with these prehistoric beasts. It's not. If you do happen to ever come across a dinosaur, you're probably doing to die.

It's Okay To Cry

Crying itself isn't bad. Cry all you want– I don't give a shit, you big baby. It's just important to recognize tears as a warning sign. If you happen to bust into a party, and everyone is crying, that's not okay. You have to get out of there. Something bad just happened and it's not going to stop when it gets to you. Chances are, someone in that party just stumbled into a classic *the-calls-are-coming-from-inside-the-house* type scenario. He or she has alerted the others to the imminent danger, and understandably killed the typical party mood. Now everyone in the house is crying and you, in full party mode, show up with hopes of finding free beer and Pringles. Selfish. Get out of the house.

Water Parks Are Fun

Water parks are NOT fun, or safe, or NOT filled with the urine and anal backwash of thousands of strangers. Water parks are the only things keeping diseases from completely dying out. Trust me. If you ride a water slide with your mouth open, you're going to die within hours.

Playing Doctor

There is no such thing as playing doctor after the age of three. Would you trust your safety with a grown man who is "playing policeman?" Nope. If someone is touching you while telling you "not to worry" because they "went to school for twelve years," make sure it was to become a doctor. You can go to school for anything these days. Get touched by someone who paid a lot of money to know how.

Bloody Nose For No Reason

Hey Tina, your random bloody noses were cute in preschool but now you have one every time you come out of some band's tour bus. Shape up or ship out. You're going to die soon.

Praise for Pooping

When you were a little tyke, everyone was super excited when you pooped. To this day, I don't think I've ever gotten that many high fives. But when you're older, and you start walking around telling people that you just pooped, expecting some kind of praise, someone is going to knock you on your ass.

Eating Mac & Cheese (Constantly)

Really bad idea. If you like the way your heart runs, you're gonna want to stop having Easy Mac for breakfast, lunch, and dinner. (Side note: you no longer have to cut your hotdogs into little pieces. I don't care how adorable it is, you could choke. I don't want to see you taken down by one-eighth of a hot dog.)

Holding Hands with Strangers

When you were little, holding hands was a great way to keep tabs on everyone. If you got lost, at least you'd get lost with someone else's kid too so your parents could console each other. Now it's just weird. Imagine being in the bank and grabbing the hand of the person next to you:

"Oh, don't worry about me. I'm not trying to rob you– I just want to make sure we don't get separated. When it's your turn to withdraw, by all means, be on your way. But for now I really think we should stick together."

Don't touch strangers. No matter how rational your decision to do so may be. Touching strangers gives them the green light to kill you. I'm pretty sure "he wouldn't let go of my hand" would hold up in court, too.

Long-Distance Relationships

I find it funny when people ask for relationship advice.

To me, giving people advice about their love life is saying pretty much anything you want, with the understanding that regardless of what you tell them they are going to do whatever the fuck they feel like doing.

After you understand *that* aspect of human nature, it becomes much more entertaining to intervene in peoples' lives. If it works out, you can be the guy who takes credit for your friends' happiness.

Oh look, a new paragraph:

Here comes a fairly bold, blanket statement: *long-distance relationships suck.*

Of course there are exceptions.

I can't stand exceptions because they tend to ruin broad, sweeping, generalizations that I like to think of as *facts*.

You do, of course, from time to time hear the story about two people who locked eyes in the hospital nursery, spending their years adding links to a romantic chain that would stretch across our nation like the backbone of the whole continent, sea to sea like the Transcontinental Railroad, overcoming all odds in a sixty-year marriage until they are buried, side by side, behind a house they built with their bare hands in Savannah, Georgia. Yes, true love *does* exist and distance cannot deter it.

Or your grandparents got married young in order to make it okay to have sex with each other. Either way.

It is my own belief that if you should find yourself contemplating a long-distance relationship, it is definitely beneficial to do so later in life. That is to say, if you are in your teens to mid-twenties, adding distance to the already baffling world of pre-love is usually a bad idea. There are always exceptions to the rule, and I realize that. And if you fall into the aforementioned demographic (babies in love, just waiting to be buried while holding hands in the South) you probably identify yourself as just that– the exception. I respect that and wish you the best of luck.

Although, for the sake of my sanity and yours, I will continue this essay without doubling back to include The Exceptions. This essay would be at least five times longer, and I don't think either of us needs *that* in our lives right now.

Time is the most valuable thing you have.

Some of you girls have bags by Coach.

Some of you boys have Beats by Dre headphones.

But *time* is the key to the most powerful aspects of life such as our memories, experience, and regret. Memories are the things that fuel the bullshit stories that you are going to tell for the rest of your life. Experiences are the overly dramatized things that actually *happened* in those stories, and regret is what you feel when you hear other people tell the stories that you wish were your own.

Your teens and twenties are a busy time. You have no idea who you are. You may think you do, but you are only beginning to scratch the surface. You are scratching yourself and it is socially acceptable. During this time you are going to meet a ton of people: school friends, teachers, coaches, parents of friends, extended family, crossing guards, whoever runs the Japanese food place in the mall, and all of these people are going to play some part in the story of your life. Sometimes you meet a person you can see yourself falling in love with (even though, at the time, you are only starting to figure out what you think that means). You then start to spend more time with that person, and thus limiting your time with others around you (the Japanese lady has forgotten your face). You have entered into a natural and often blissful series of events. Sometimes your blossoming love moves away. Maybe her gender-ambiguous parent finds a better job across the country in Blout County Alabama, working in covered bridge restoration, or your small town suddenly becomes war-torn, whatever the case may be, distance has been created between you and your new mouth-kissing partner. Summer nights spent gallivanting around the neighborhood have become summer nights laying on your stomach and kicking your feet behind you on the telephone. Even worse, you could be spending even *more* of your time on the computer instead of learning about what warm nighttime air tastes like. (It's delicious. It's like hot chocolate mixed with the smell of freshly cut grass.)

Sacrificing your time and experiences earlier in your life often leads to an assload of regret as you get older. You start putting yourself in a position to miss out on new things. Nighttime air aside, you *could* be frenching the entire block if the mood strikes you. As you get older, you could be discovering how awesome it is to be good at sex by using the very motto your parents taught you during your tee ball years: "practice makes perfect."

These are your formative years.

You should be making mistakes and molding yourself into a person who knows right from wrong like the back of your hand because you have been to the top of the mountain and rolled, violently, down the other side.

You made a girl cry by pretending to be asleep when she asks you if you love her.

You made a boy cry by pretending to be asleep when a he asks you out for coffee.

You've been thrown out of a high school football game for fondling your girlfriend under the bleachers.

You've been thrown out of a bar for making out with a beautiful Dominican girl in a public bathroom (Related: you now know how fucking disgusting it is to fool around with someone in a public bathroom).

Youth is a big, dumb, stupid, loud party, where everyone inside is screaming at the top of their lungs and tripping all over themselves on their way out the door. Everyone is in a rush to leave and no one knows why. Long-distance relationship people are the ones upstairs online with their significant other, hoping the party will just quiet down for a few minutes.

But alas– there is no one piece of advice I could dispense that would be right for *everyone* on the cusp of a long-distance relationship. And I'm fine with that. After all, who the fuck am I to tell *you* what to do?

There are people, unlike me, who are not as interested in making the same kind of mistakes and taking unnecessary risks in order to shape who they will become. There are people who were born to meet one person and fall in love.

They hear the metaphorical party raging downstairs, turn, smile, and make sure everyone who comes together leaves together.

Get your everyday philosophy-type-bullshit game up.

From Page to Screen: The 90's

Everyone knows that when books are turned into movies they usually lose some of their luster. Here are a few movies from the 90's where the book was most *definitely* better. *

10 Things I Hate About You

Tank Girl

Jury Duty

Jurassic Park

Armageddon

Beverly Hills Ninja

Wild Wild West

Home Alone

Schindler's List

Goodfellas

Happy Gilmore

Three Kings

Babe

The Full Monty

The Last of the Mohicans

101 Dalmatians

Starship Troopers

*I really have no idea if any of these were ever *actually* books.
Except *Jurassic Park*. That was definitely a book.

Stop Crying About the Music Industry

People love to complain about the state of the music industry. These people often come with quirky catch phrases such as, "Man, music isn't what it used to be." No shit. Very few things are exactly as they used to be. Rocks and dirt have pretty good staying power, but other than that, things tend to change with the times. "What happened to MUSIC?" says the fifteen year-old in the *Dark Side of the Moon* crew-neck tee shirt. "Music today is nothing like it was in the 60's." Really? That's what you're going to go with? Because you're fifteen. You, yourself are nothing like you were in the 60's.

My guess is, people form these bitter opinions based on what they see in popular culture. I.e. what's popular on the radio, TV, and so on. They see people like Chris Brown and Taylor Swift at the Grammys and say, "This is what music is now." Unfortunately, these people have formed their opinions based on the easiest information to come by. People who are bitter about the music industry have made their statement based on what has been fed to them. As a human being with taste buds I know that when I am fed something I don't particularly enjoy, I seek fulfillment elsewhere.

Today, we are lucky enough to have the Internet. On the Internet one can find countless alternatives to what is fed to you by the mainstream media. There are thousands upon thousands of people creating and re-creating art. The state of music is alive and well, you just have to meet them halfway and make an effort to find it. Most people don't do that. Most people hear whatever happens to be on at the time and make a judgment. The "state of the music industry" is happening down the street from you every weekend in clubs, coffee houses, and dive bars. I realize I'm not giving you too much credit, but I'm gonna say you are too lazy to go check it out. * (Though if I am wrong, and you frequent local shows, support local artists, and STILL find time to complain about the music industry, I will apologize to you personally. Tweet me at @mikefalzone.)

Let's say after you read this little essay, maybe a week down the line, you catch yourself complaining about music. Great. You have used your brainpower to form an opinion and I am proud of you for doing so. Thoughts evoke emotions, and emotions evoke action. Thoughts are what we in the "business" call Step One. Step Two would be to go create something yourself, or throw your support behind like-minded people who do.

Complaining followed by a lack of any type of productive action is always shitty. Whether it's about something important like politics, or something *really* important, like what your mother made for dinner last night. "Mom this split-pea soup is mediocre at BEST! You make is every night and I am sick of it! Do I want *what*? Dessert? No! I'm all filled up on your craptastic soup!"

This scenario doesn't seem right, does it? No. If you don't like your mother's cooking, you grab a cookbook and a whisk and you show that bitch what's up. And don't call your mother a bitch, please.

Like rap but hate Nicki Minaj? Fine. (You're missing out, but fine.) Name three rappers in your town. Did you go to their last show? No? Oh. Hate dubstep? Great. Love dubstep? Super. Are you confused as to why so many people hate it? Do you care? You shouldn't. Listen to whatever you like on repeat, in an unapologetic fashion, until your ears bleed. Finding things you like is amazing.

If you do decide to create something of your own, my hat is off to you. Good for you for putting yourself out there. You may suck for a little while but if you love it, it won't matter. Just keep doing it. I believe it was John Mayer who said, "Write compared to nothing." The best way to make an impact is to write what the world is missing. Create what you wish someone else would have but didn't. Make something that you could love and then do just that, love it. It sure beats complaining about problems you do nothing to solve.

* I made a video about this subject and put it on YouTube. A very nice computer programmer left the following comment in direct opposition to my previous statement:

People act on plenty of their complaints... just not the ones they aren't fully interested in. I work in computer networking, and I work in a hospital. I dislike Ke$ha greatly and feel she is a bad influence. Do I do anything about it? NO I'm busy as hell doing things I consider more worth my time. Does that mean my opinion on Ke$ha is invalid? No, it just means I have a complaint, and don't spend all my free time trying to fix everything I dislike. "Musician dislikes Firefox? Learn to program!"

First of all, I love this comment. This guy/gal is great and they make an excellent point. However, what I'm saying is:

1. No one is saying your opinion is invalid (see above).
2. Have more important things to do? Great. Do them and stop wasting your time talking about Ke$ha, I promise she doesn't talk about you.
3. See argument code-named: Operation Support People Who

Create What You Like Instead of Sitting Back and Crying About The People Who Don't.

4. "Musician dislikes Firefox? Learn to program!" Or... don't use Firefox.

The 15 Worst Things to Do With Glitter

1. Hide it in a tube of toothpaste

2. Use it as lubricant

3. Mix it with water and freeze

4. Throw it at stranger's faces

5. Mix it with your dad's pipe tobacco

6. Pack it into a snorkel

7. Use it to wean you off of cocaine

8. Touch it

9. Lie about where you got it

10. Pay for it

11. Leave a trail to or from your apartment with it

12. Gargle with it

13. Throw it out of a car window

14. Cover condolence cards in it

15. Put it in any envelope mailed in 2001

The 15 Best Things to do with Glitter

1. Cover yourself in it before a fight

2. Blow it into your roommate's face as soon as they wake up

3. Sprinkle it onto a paper plate covered in craft glue

4. Cover the toilet seat at your office with it

5. Cover bad report cards in it

6. Arts

7. Crafts

8. Fill piñatas with it without telling anyone

9. Wear a prom dress and a set of wings out in public and try to pay for things with it

10. Fill a telescope with glitter and make your own kaleidoscope

11. Glue it to the front of your ex-girlfriend's new TV

12. Tape it to your teeth and run around saying you're a toothpaste commercial

13. Feed it to a horse and watch it turn into a unicorn

14. Replace the contents of a Pixy Stick with it

15. Swallow a cup of glitter minutes before your tonsillectomy

(They will thank you when you come to)

The Universe Doesn't Owe You Anything

I personally think the only thing you are truly *owed* is the chance to explain yourself after you've done something ridiculously stupid. I have done enough stupid shit to know I wasn't acting in the same way I normally would. At this point in human evolution, I believe we are all fully formed and functional human beings. If one of us should do something classified as *less than smart*, we should have the opportunity to apologize and let everybody know that it was a mere lapse in judgment. In other words, we do stupid things and try hard not to be the product of our actions (which may be ultimately stupid after all).

Remember that time in the TGI Friday's bathroom when you peed in the garbage can after happy hour? That was stupid and inconsiderate, but I know it wasn't something you'd normally do. However, if the aforementioned stupidity cannot be easily explained away, or if it is repeated, we can then simply classify you as dumb. Quietly awaiting the next round of elimination. It's hard to shed a justified label like that. That's the guy who pees in trash cans. He's dumb.

Keep in mind that just because someone is able to explain away his most recent idiocy, this does not mean the rest of us need to automatically forgive him. We will merely recognize the self-awareness of the idiot in question and nod silently. You are owed a chance to explain yourself, once, that's it. This is where the universe's debt to you ends. (I do, however, feel I am owed unlimited data. My virginity was lost to my first cell phone contract.)

Let us examine the Universe's outstanding debt to the human race as it pertains to interpersonal and romantic relationships. Why? Because if I hear "I'm ready to settle down, but I cannot find him/her" one more time, I'm going to lay on my back and throw up until what ever day it happens to be ends, and whatever day is next, starts. I am annoyed by the immediate need we have to satisfy our cravings the instant they pop into existence. Regardless of what you want, life is going to keep happening. Shut up and roll with it.

You are ready to settle down... great. You've done the work. You are relatively happy with yourself, you have played and then mopped up the field; you are ready. You are done with the riff-raff, the periphery, the "periff-a-raff."

Now, get this though your head: Just because you feel as though you are ready to settle down, the universe is not obligated to hand you your future. "Here is your mate, go forth and procreate... make 'em cute," says the universe. This doesn't happen.

Lots of people say they don't want to go hook up. Fine. There are pros and cons to hooking up. Cons: it can be relatively icky out there. I'll bypass the list of contractible diseases and substitute it with a phrase my father said to me once: "You're do-jig is gonna fall off." Other than that, the romantic truth behind hooking up is that the more you put yourself out there in a vulnerable position, the more likely you are to be broken (or bruised, at minimum).

Pros: Hooking up is fun. At the very least, you've just earned yourself a few good stories. The strongest argument in my book for hooking up is idea that in order to meet "the one," you must first meet "a bunch." It's like when you go the Chili's, and order a sampler platter. Everything is fried and you know it's bad for you, but it helps you put things in perspective and decide what you'd really like. Although, I feel like most of the time you go into dinner already knowing what you'd really like, and then find any excuse to fill yourself with the garbage anyway. Whatever. Toss a celery stick in once in a while, you'll be all right. I'll stick by that until life experience proves me wrong.

Maybe that wasn't clear. I know what I wanted to say but now I'm just thinking about chicken fingers.

At some point you are going to venture out into the world (preferably in the rain for dramatic purposes), and you're going to spread your arms out wide, look up to the heavens and say, "I'M READY FOR LOVE NOW," as though you are ordering from some omnipotent drive thru window. "What time is it? Three? Ok, I'll have a late lunch, then just a bit of unconditional love please." Selfish.

Bypassing this one-sided conversation with the sky is simple, and one of the biggest favors you can do for yourself in life is to be happy. I'm not talking about the "I left the center bite of the cheese burger for last" kind of happy. I'm talking about true contentment with yourself. I don't think you can separate true happiness and self-confidence.

Let's play a little game I like to call, "Peep this Math." A human being who is one hundred percent happy with who they are can still only bring fifty percent of what is needed to be in a happy relationship. In other words, in order to "form a more perfect union," you must first be sure that your own house is not divided against itself. Being one hundred percent satisfied with yourself equals fifty percent of what it takes to be in a happy relationship. You bring your fifty percent, I'll bring mine, and we'll cross our fingers and hope we don't get divorced at some point.

Stop wasting time whining about being ready to love and just be awesome on your own. It will work out, you have to have faith. And shut up... never stop shutting up.

Tweets From the Twelve Year-Old Across the Street

The following is a selection of my favorite tweets from the kid who lives across the street from me. My advice is to not read too far into any one of these. Love them for the charming morsels of adolescent wisdom that they are. Enjoy.

Going somewhere around 2:00

Some times people act wierd like there acting

It's a pain to wake up every day

US Army is beastly

I wish @robdyrdek was at my house to skateboard that would be awesome

It would be so awesome if I won 999 million dollars

Haven't done cards in a long time

Foot ball is my thing

9:59 may be back on twitter

What ever it takes don't give up

My head hurts some times but I really don't know why not from head eggs

Trying to do a trick takes time

Need to do weight lifting

I thought some jack ass broke in my window

Fuck Adolf hiter

Sort of miss the old days

Having teachers breathe on you it's sort of crazy how they do that

If it was funny to have a cake fight I would

Thinking what to tomorrow

Some times of you want to buy something you don't have the money for it

Just saw some kid fall down my stairs

If our time was 2:00pm right now that would be weird

Teachers bug me

Having to much snacks makes you fat

If one of your friends did not know how to skateboard but instead he throws it

My room is really not that big

no one knows what heaven looks like

Virginity

Losing your virginity is not as big a deal as it's made out to be in every romantic teen comedy movie. In reality, it's more like uncovering a new way to disappoint the people closest to you.

Losing your virginity turns every romantic courtship you'll have in the future into a sort of job interview. If you find yourself with too much experience, you won't get hired. If you have too little experience, your prospective employer will tell their friends about you and laugh. It's a Catch-22: by the time you meet the company you'd like to spend your time making love to, you want to have a firm grasp on the sexual SOP without looking like a whore on your resume. (You'd think "the oldest profession" would be held in a higher regard when it comes to job experience. It's not.)

People talk about losing their virginity the same way they would talk about winning a race. "I did it! Did you do it? You gotta do it by prom! I'm pretty sure your junk goes bad if you don't do it by prom!"

It's a lot like being the first kid that could do a pull-up in third grade: everyone is jealous of that kid but at the same time no one really knows why. My friend Jeff could do seventy-five pull-ups in third grade. He also had a stomach full of abs... in THIRD GRADE. What the hell are you doing everyone morning that you have abs in third grade? A huge part of me still hates him for that.

Sex, at least in the beginning, is a lot like learning to play the piano; you are not going to be good at it for years, and you practice obsessively by yourself while trying not to wake up your parents. Many times people feel pressured into having sex (and playing piano). Nine times out of ten, the person pressuring you into intercourse is horrible at it. You're going to want to shy away from those people. There is no redeeming quality in a person that pressures another human being into sex. You'll never hear anyone say, "Yeah, he put a lot of pressure on me to sleep with him... but he's really close with his family." That's not real.

One of the many cool things about your body is that you can do what you want with it. More importantly, you *don't do* what you *don't want* with it. Having a baby and getting an STD are both outcomes of the same choice. How about that? Do your best to not make that choice in the back of an SUV. Babies are awesome. They are tiny people. A good rule of thumb when raising a child is that you'd like them to have a good story behind their conception. Here is a good example of a horrible story to tell your child when she asks how she came to be:

"Well, your dad could throw a football really far and I just seemed to run out of self-esteem by the time I met him... so... here you are!"

Take your time and make sure your kid has a solid story behind it. Something cool and thought- provoking. Treat your offspring like an X-Men character. Make sure you can write an entire graphic novel behind its origin.

Once you finally do have sex, you're just going to be confused about it for a while. It's like the first time you see "Inception." Everyone is talking about it like they love it so much, and you can't stop trying to figure out why the ending didn't go the way you thought it would. And like everything else, it gets better the more you screw it up. Small pun intended.

What Your First-Date Food Choice Says About You

Grilled Cheese: Says you still rely on your mother for everything.

Mac and Cheese: You are not willing to put more than three minutes of effort into anything.

Buffalo Wings: I couldn't care less how I look to you right now.

Ordering a sandwich without anything it usually comes with: Says even you are out of your league.

Pulled Pork Sandwich: A shameless reference to your masturbation addiction

Spaghetti: I couldn't care less how I look to you right now.

Twenty-Piece Chicken Nugget Meal: Why are you even there right now?

Anything in Slider Form: You are not even confident enough to use utensils.

Tofu Pot Pie: You're just trying to prove you know what tofu is.

Dessert First: You live by your own set of rules.

You're Not invited to the Wedding Because You're Acting Like a Tool

I'm at the point in my life where all of my friends are getting married. Not me though (always the bridesmaid). This recent phenomenon has separated the people I know into two groups: the "about to be wed," and the "incredibly selfish and stupid." Group one tends to have certain characteristics, such as a job and an overall plan. Group two will identify themselves with the battle cry: "I never see ___ anymore!" If the layman heard the battle cry in passing conversation, one may think the subject is becoming an evil person, disregarding friends and family alike in a whirling dervish of lameness and love. In reality, they are getting their shit together. That's the thing about plans: they're made of up several steps that need to be taken in order to be completed successfully.

I can only assume that the accuser just sobered up from whatever they have been doing for the past few months. The accuser rubs his or her eyes, is disgusted by their morning breath, and wonders when life fell out of sync. "Steve never comes around anymore to watch sports ball on Sundays. Bit of a dick, Steve is."

Wrong again, sleepy.

Steve is picking out the color of his tie for the wedding. Guess who's not in the wedding party? You. You're an asshole. Leave it to you to take a significant moment in your friend's life and turn it around to be about how lame you are.

This is what happens: someone meets somebody else, they fall in love, and start a new life. You may have heard of two other people doing that recently, and if they didn't, you wouldn't be here right now. Sometimes love doesn't even need to be part of the equation. Sex does, but they make other, well-written books about that kind of thing. Maybe just accept that this is the way shit goes and deal with it accordingly. Take a step outside yourself and react like an actual friend would.

The worst thing you can do in this situation is remain an asshole. Remain steadfast with your guilt-trips and so on.

Let's flash back to high school for a second. No matter who you are, you have a ton of friends. There are really no "losers" anymore. Have you realized this? Losers just seek out other losers and band together, making them popular in a separate but equally sweaty circle of teenage angst. If you're lucky enough to go to college, you'll find much of the same. Tons of people. Most are wondering around, seeking out their own. The only difference from high school is that you tend to hook up with (or throw up on) *more* of these people. Very few of these friends will stay with you forever. Sometimes we lose sight of how lucky we are to know people for such an extended period of time. Do yourself a favor and recognize how these relationships change over time so you are not left in the dust as you grow up. It's not always going to be you and your buddy on the couch playing video games. It's not always going to be you and your girlfriends, sitting criss-cross applesauce, playing Mall Madness (or whatever girls do for fun).

At some point you meet the person you'd like to spend the rest of your life with and your friends start to dwindle in numbers. People fall out of touch with one another. This is natural. This is the evolution of your friends. Darwin says, "Most of your friends are stupid. Keep walking upright and you'll be fine." He's right, always. What a guy. The accuser sets these actions in motion by complaining to or about the people trying to get their lives together. Do so and you become the first person to be left behind.

Planning a wedding? Three hundred dollars a plate? Hmmm, who can we afford to leave out of our extravagant steak-eating party? Well, Cindy has been kind of an asshole. NICE! Cut eight more people and we can get that chocolate fountain!

My guess is that this doesn't apply to everyone. I understand that some of you are in high school now. You are seeing your friends spend more time with their brand new boyfriends or girlfriends. You get upset because your friend's new love interest is kind of an idiot. That's probably true. In you friend's defense, they may say, "Well, my parents were high school sweethearts, and that's going to happen to us. I don't need friends as long as I have Billy. He doesn't like when I call him Billy, but I do it anyway." Real quick: Billy is probably cheating on you. Sorry.

In conclusion, don't be an asshole. Your friends need more than just you. You were great for a while, and I'm sure you still are, to a certain extent. Your friends need financial stability, a house, unconditional love, food, bi-weekly sexual intercourse, one of those gum containers that fit in your car's cup holder and a laundry list of other things you probably can't provide when you are coming down on them for being grown up. What about you? Maybe you need someone new in your life! Get on one of them Internet dating sites. Start "poking" and "winking" the shit out of everyone you see.

Nope. Not everyone.

Worst Email Subject Lines to Get From Your Significant Other

DO NOT FREAK OUT...

We need to talk

FWD: 14 ways to know he's definitely cheating on you

I know you told me not to but...

I found this link about PUPPIES!!!

I'm on way home right now!

FWD: $1495 one bedroom w/fireplace!!!!

This is not cheating...

This would be good for us! Http://...

FWD: This is why I didn't want you to teach my father how to
    use the Internet!

You're Never Gonna Find Love

It's hard to find true love. I often find that the biggest obstacle standing in a person's way is himself, so I have come up with a simple list of things that can help you recognize and rectify habits that may be keeping you from finding your one true match.

Some list-makers simply take a "set it and forget it" approach to list making. They jot down a few general ideas and leave you out in the wild to fend for yourself. Below, you will see that I have beefed up my list with simple explanation to help you on your way to happiness. Should you feel as though you need some more explaining, feel free to tweet me @mikefalzone. If I think I can answer your question in 140 characters or less, I will. If not, I will continue doing whatever I'm doing.

The following is a list of reasons why you will never find love. Enjoy.

You're wearing a wedding dress in your online dating profile picture

Really? That's the picture you are going to post to help you meet the man of your dreams? Unless your profile says,

"Never married. I just bought this dress because it was on sale. I consider this purchase to be an adorably preemptive response to our eventual courtship," then after that try adding, "I swear I'm not fucking crazy." Good luck.

If you are still wearing hats with ripped brims and cargo shorts

Nothing screams Lonely College Guy louder than this pathetic uniform. If you are wearing a baseball hat, I'm going to assume you are on a baseball team. Congratulations, being an athlete is difficult and you must have a demanding training regimen. If you are not on (or currently coaching) a baseball team, please remove your baseball hat.

Furthermore, should you choose to wear the hat, and should that hat be ripped in the front, you will appear to be wearing garbage. Please remove all garbage from your head. The cargo shorts are out, too. Don't be afraid to try and wear a color. If you spend your life wearing earthy tones, you are going to blend in with the earth until you are buried in it.

If you follow everything you say with eight or more A's

This usually comes from girls who seemed to be starved for attention. Holding out the last syllable of any word requires a minimal level of concentration and a maximum level of breath control. A needy thirteen to twenty-five year-old female is not unlike a needy infant in this way. A baby needs a bottle as an annoying girl needs to be acknowledged. Here are some key phrases where eight or more A's are tacked on to an otherwise A-less word in the hopes that the speaker gains an audience:

"Oh-em-gee you guyz! What are we even DOING tonighttttaaaaaaaa!?"

"Billy, did you SEE?! I bought a new skirt and you're not even lookeeeeennnnaaaaaaaa!"

"The bitch threw up ALL OVER MeeeeaaaaaaAAaaaa"

Before we move on, let's throw the people who CaPiTaLiZe every other letter in the things they type into this category as well. The way I see it, this is the text-based equivalent to adding A's. It's just as annoying. Whenever I see random capital letters, I am forced to read what is being typed in the dumb girl voice.

Example:

*****ToNiTe iS tHa NITE! MaRtiNis WiTh mY BeStIeS!*****

If you are one of those people at the bar who screams whenever a new song comes on

I usually determine where I want to stand at a bar based on the location of these people. Oh the screamers are by the bar? Yeah, I'm not really thirsty tonight. They usually form crop circles around each other and are often found pointing upward with their forefinger and pinky as the DJ changes tracks.

Signature phrases:

"OHHHHHH!"

"THIS IS MY SONG!"

"THIS IS MY SHIT!"

"THIS SHIT IS MY JAM!"

"THIS JAM IS THE SHIT!"

And so on.

No one needs you to scream when a new song comes on. 1) Anyone with ears is aware that the song has changed. Even the deaf guy touching the subwoofers hates these people. 2) No one cares if this is your favorite song. I swear to God.

Oh man, this one particular girl loves "Super Bass," I'm gonna go by her a drink. Maybe I'll take her out to dinner. I can't wait to tell our kids how we met: Kids, your mother's four-hundred dollar shoes smelled like vomit so I wasn't going to talk to her, but then "Super Bass" came on! She threw her hands in the air and spilled half her vodka cranberry on herself. That's when I knew we would have a beautiful baby boy and name him Nichols.

If every sentence you speak goes up at the end, as if you are asking a question? (Don't worry Canada, you're safe. We'll keep this one domestic.)

You should have learned how to stop yourself from doing this by the summer going into pre-school. If you are not asking a question, your voice shouldn't end on the up-swing.

Typical Conversation with an Up-swinger:

Up-swinger: I went to the movies? And then I saw my brother? And he was with his new girlfriend? It was pretty weird?

ME: ...What?

Please speak correctly. If you do this long enough, no one is going to have any idea whether or not you are asking a question.

If you still go tanning:

Tanning has been proven a thousand times over to cause cancer and make your skin look like the thing Indiana Jones uses keep his whip attached to his belt. If smoking is a turn off, tanning should be no different. Turning yourself orange isn't attractive. No one wants to fuck a Lorax.

If you know you're pretty:

This one is very specific. Everyone should know that they are pretty; the problem lies in how intensely you choose to deal with this information. In my experience the "pretty" girls in middle school or high school tend to not talk to the guys they may very well end up marrying. There is a status divide. This particular list item has more to do with my childhood hang-ups than day-to-day life. I would apologize, but this is my book. I thought about removing this one, but then I didn't. If anything I would change the wording to read, "If you know you're pretty, don't be an asshole."

If you give your dog a middle name:

It's a dog. I'll make you a deal: if your dog can pronounce its first or last name, you can give it a middle name. Deal? Let's say that you bring a first date back to your place. Great job, you're making moves. Then your adorable canine heartbreak safety net runs up to greet your new friend:

POTENTIAL RELATIONSHIP: Oh, who's this?

YOU: This is Fluffy Margaret Petingale. Say hi Fluffy! Say HI Fluffy Margaret!

POTENTIAL RELATIONSHIP: (Door Slam)

If you abbreviate speech:

You were blessed with a tongue and a brain. Use both of those things in conjunction with one another and say real words. Here is a short list of words you should never abbreviate (unless of course you are making fun of someone who just did).

Crazy > Cray

Totally > Toates

Obviously > Obvy

Oh my God > Oh-em-Gee

Hahaha > LoL

Gorgeous > Gorge

If you like Chex Mix more than dating:

I was really into Chex Mix at the time I wrote this. I am not endorsed by them in anyway. I'd like to get that out of the way sooner than later. What a terrific snack. Chex Mix is a bag of delicious diversity. Eighty percent of the time, I would choose that over awkward sexual interaction.

If you suggest that we change the words of the National Anthem because your favorite celebrity fucked it up:

No mercy on this one. The song was written in 1814 and is sung before roughly EVERYTHING that happens. You learn the lyrics when you are six, you grow up to be a professional singer, and then someone pays you to sing the National Anthem at the Super Bowl. Don't fuck it up.

No Excuses. You memorized the lyrics to the Justin Beiber song that came out last week. You "don't even like" Justin Beiber. Check yourself.

If you force people into commitment:

You have probably learned by now that what you say to a person may very well change the way they act. What you need to understand now is that what you say will rarely change the way that someone feels. If somebody truly changes their viewpoint on something, it's because they have seen a larger associated downside associated with their previous way of thinking. Changing the way you feel about something is the outcome of an internal discussion.

If you refuse to commit:

…Seriously, you have to grow up at some point.

Backward by Craig D'Andrea

Truth be told, I did not like Mike Falzone when I first met him. As the story goes, we were both opening for some blue-eyed flash in the pan with a huge head named Teddy Geiger at The Webster in Hartford, Connecticut. I had driven to the show with our soon-to-be mutual friend Jimmy because he also thought that if he opened for someone like T. Geigs he would be on the fast track to fame. We all did. That was a large miscalculation on our parts. After the show, Jimmy and I drove and talked. Mostly we talked about how awful it was to play in front of two hundred thirteen-year-old girls but we also discussed Mike.

I am the type of person who is hesitant to open up to strangers most of the time even though I am good at talking about nothing with anyone. Michael Falzone is not like me. I found him irritating and stupid. Really stupid. He had a chinstrap beard and played stupid acoustic singer/songwriter music that was, as it always is, laced with the need to succeed. There was no way I would ever try to see him again.

Fast-forward many months and Jimmy and I find ourselves playing open mic nights in Connecticut which inevitably leads us to another chance meeting with our co-opener. (Side note: At this point Teddy Geiger is nowhere to be found.) We know that I had already formed my opinions but at this point I thought giving people second chances was a good idea so I gave Mike another one. As I write this I'm guessing that Mike probably thought I was an asshole after our first meeting so he was probably thinking the same thing. During these open mics I decided that Mike was probably one of the funniest people I had ever met although I never admitted that to him or Jimmy. I was playing hard to get.

Fast forward another set of months and the three of us are real friends. We go on trips together to visit New York City and the metropolitan powerhouse that is Hartford, Connecticut. There is texting, manly kisses (Jimmy and Mike), a very high level of sarcasm, and many insensitive text messages that had topics too awful to repeat. Every time we got together it was almost like each of us wanted to make the other laugh. Knowing that you have the power to make Mr. Falzone laugh is one of the greatest powers on earth.

Upon being asked to write a Foreword for this book, and I use the term *book* loosely, I was flattered but nervous. I accepted on the condition that I would only write an Epilogue. Still nervous. Could I do a Mike Falzone book justice? I could try. I have seen the YouTube videos, I have even helped write some of the jokes in them, I have been to his apartment and been ignored while he was making fun of thirteen year-old kids while playing Call of Duty, and I have been judged by my friend. The only essay I read before writing this was *Long-Distance Relationships* and it held a special place in my heart.

I met my current girlfriend on tour in Kansas City, Missouri last year and when I got back home I found myself explaining the story of how she and I met to Mike while recording music and jokes in my basement studio. As soon as I finished the story he looked at me like I was a fucking idiot. His eyes were saying "You're a fucking idiot," and so was his mouth. But beneath his lack of outward compassion there was some part of him who was happy for me. Fuck you Mike for doubting me but thank you for being honest. I'm still with her and surprisingly enough, she likes him.

In closing, I would like to say that even though Mike thinks he has all of the answers he is a good person no matter what you think of his videos and music. They might suck but they are honest. I have learned a lot from his insights and view of the world and I try to apply them to my life when I run out of logical decisions. Yes, he may play video games and wear sweatpants most of the time but he is talented, smart and cute. I hope you took his advice. Advice like that might really help someone like you. In closing I would like to say that Mike Falzone has never met my family and that he really is full of shit. Ham on a couch.

Acknowledgements

Hi, this is Mike. I'm not going to try to tell you anything about myself in this little paragraph because I just spent a whole book doing that. You're probably tired of it by now. Instead, I'd like to take this opportunity to acknowledge Anne Christianson, who convinced me that this project wasn't just something I was doing because "I thought it would be funny;" Craig D'Andrea, for helping me with some of these lists and telling me what a shitty person I am; Shandy Lawson, for his time and talent; Rob Dobi for finally working with me on something; Kickstarter, for making this whole thing possible; and YouTube for doing what YouTube does.

Special thanks to:

Shandy Lawson
Rob Dobi
Craig D'Andrea
Meghan Tonjes
James Thompson
Jim McLoughlin
Lee Warren
Paweł Kostyk
Meagan Harman
Simon Asher

Stephen Siegel

Sarah "POOOOOOST" Simmons

Shane Bridges

Elea Guywiththehair Tsentzelis

Taylor Jackson

Mitchell Collins

Karen Polito

Melissa Mulligan

Mollie Hantman-Weill

Brittany Pala

OpheliaDagger

Eli Strong

T Nichols

Dave Piel

Travis Helwig

Jenny Jaffe

Mom & Dad

Michael Buckley

Anne Christianson

4229884R00058

Made in the USA
San Bernardino, CA
05 September 2013